Confessions poetry collection
Volume 1

Emmanuel Wallace

~Table of contents~

-society speaks
1.To be verified-**5**
2.His Darkness-**8**
3.Heartless Society-**11**
4.Patient-**13**
5.Why life-**15**
6.Lost-**16**
7.Cut Off-**18**
8. Success?-**20**
9.L.O.V.E-**23**
-Nature speaks
1. The Branchless Tree-**26**
2.The Thistle and Thorn-**28**
3.Desert of Green-**29**
-intermixed
1.Dreamer-**32**
2.River of Dreams-**34**
3.Silly Dream-**36**
4.A Loner's Dream-**39**
5.colors-**41**
6.status-**43**
7.internal bout-**45**
8. Idk-**47**

<u>Open Your eyes….</u>

<u>For when one confesses they….</u>

<u>Might catch you slipping…</u>

Society Speaks

<u>To be verified</u>

To be verified
Just let me clarify
That i have to lose to gain
Endure the world's greatest pain
Rejection.
Just to be accepted
Left in the shadows with the rest
I always claimed i was blessed
Instead my life has turned into one huge mess.
Pain
I've been seen as lame
Since the beginning I've been the same
I guess my breakthrough never came
To be verified
Let me clarify
That I need 100k
Just to feel sane
Everyone says the greatest feeling in the world
Is fame
Then why do I feel so drained
What have I really gained
Who can I blame
Me
I allowed myself to drown in this emotional
Sea

Lost in a void I can't escape
To breathe
To be verified
Let me clarify
I have to change to
Blend
A lot of people say n***as ain't
You already know
But where does that leave me
I just want to be
Free
To be verified
Let me clarify
I must lie just so my feed isn't
Dry
Lost looking through someone else's
Eyes
To be verified
Let me clarify
First I must be tossed aside
In my pain I'm forced to reside
Blind.
To be verified?

Disclaimer: there is nothing wrong with being verified… it's in that moment state of why or what you strive to be verified for. First verify yourself then let the world decide...they can't hurt you if you place a shield of confidence before you. We're all special, let's make our impact known whether we are verified for our stupidity, kindness, motivationalism, interest,wisdom, etc. whatever it be let it shine accept the opportunities because they often only come once. Take it the first time and don't let it pass you by twice.
TO BE VERIFIED

His Darkness

Look me in the eyes and tell me what you see.
Do you see an empty vessel that fights daily?
Fighting to finally realize what it means to be
free.
In a society that claims around my people it's
best to flee.
My life never started on a clean sheet.
My people...Me!
Were captured by men of your fleets!
No disrespect but your insults attack me
internally!
You say different skin color brings forth
Different levels of prosperity
The difference?...You see, it shines quite
glaringly.
When you look at me, what do you really see?
Do you think I don't have dreams?
Do you think I don't know what love means?
Do you think I'm a man who doesn't want to
see,
His child beam,
With happiness and joy knowing his father has
seen
Him go on to do great things?
What you may think, is I'm all about the bling,

Or what I like to call money…that chingaling.
That idea...let me just say that's a tragedy;
But because this has become my people's
reality,
You look at me like I should be doing the same
thing.
And let me tell you, that stings!
Look me in the eyes and tell me what you
really see.
You know what, what does that even mean?
Here I'll tell you and it'll be nice and clean.
Three lines is all I need!
Listen to what i say and trust me,
Being black isn't as bad as it seems
In my darkness much light does it bring
When i chase my dreams with a full head of
steam
You may laugh because being black, not every
light is green,
But trust me, that's the best thing!
Because deep down it's motivating!
Because through darkness, no matter what it
may be,
Once the light shines
It shall be seen
Society says when you see me it's best to flee.
But listen, before you run
Make sure you know exactly what you see.

Look me in the eyes and tell me what *you* really see.

Heartless society

Is that really what we want to be?
A place where we make others feel
The need
To hide their identity
Make others feel like peasants
At the lower level of the
"Social hierarchy"
Make others hate the things
they loved in the beginning
Elapsed time
One
Two
Three
Heartless society
Is that really where we want to be?
A place where we suffocate each other
To the point where none of us can breathe
A place where hatred and fear is king
A place where you can't be clean
To succeed
A place where we force each other to be
A perfect piece, in the puzzle of
our ideologies
Heartless society
What do you even bring?

Hatred
Fear
Loss of identity
Suffocation
Man, that stings
Heartless society
Is that really where we want to be?
A heartless society.

<u>Patient</u>

This is crazy
Never would I have expected this
To happen to me
It's affected my life in so many
Categories
I fear sooner or later I'll forget to
Breathe
Please pray for me
I feel it will uplift my spirits
Mightily
Aaaaah so much pain does this place
bring
I wish I were back home
Free
Look at me; it's impossible to stop
Crying
I know this is a test, sent from above just for
Me
It's not about whether my
Body
Fails or
Succeeds
It's about, through the process
Will I believe?

Through it all a better life I will
Redeem
In this bed, everything seems sketchy
But I do decree
No matter how much I
Bleed
How afraid I
Seem
Despite how dark the
Things
That fill my head with all kinds of
Possibilities
May be
That light at the end of the tunnel I can
See
And once again hopefully I shall be
Free
I
Believe
This is what a patient
Thinks.

<u>Why life?</u>

<u>In the mind of those rejected</u>

Hiding from life.
Sigh
Why does it always make *me*
Cry?
Why can't I just say goodbye?
I'm sick and tired of all the lies.
All the petty binds,
All the foolish crimes.
I just want to hide.
Stay inside.
Stay alive.
But still, I am stuck in this abyss
Called time.
Struggling to find the right rhymes.
To tell you what's on my mind.
Tell you how I feel.
I don't have a shield.
I can't chill.
I don't possess that pill.
My mind is like a grill,
Constantly used but always off.
It feels like life had a cough and I just so
happened To miss the right spot.
Listen.

Lost

Kneeling I tremble
Staring at my hands
Within is something beating
It's my heart
I surrender
Away i toss it into a field
The field of many hearts forgot
Lost.
But at what cost
I wish the pain would stop
This emptiness inside is deafening
I have no energy left in me
What do i believe
Who am I
Lost
Afraid i try to fade
In the background, no shade
Exposed a voice sounds from above
full of compassion and love
I listened for the voice of the man above
He told me to come
his hand outstretched
I felt a complete mess
What do I have left
Lost
I followed his hand closely
According to the path ahead
I saw where I first bled
The field where left my heart

Right from the start
The hand moved into the field
I asked god,
lord
Is it real
He answered saying
Yes it will be okay
You won't be too late
I followed his hand in search for my heart
Lost.
now I stand,
heart still beating in the sand
I scooped it to my hand
And to the ground i fall
listening to it's beckoning call
Kneeling once again
I ask
lord
where do I begin
In that very moment he said
stand
Take your heart and be made whole again
Be made complete
I will set you free
I believe you are no longer lost
You are *found*
Safe and sound
Lost.

<u>Cut-Off</u>

Why do we cut each other off?
Sometimes it's for nothing at all.
Someone just wants to talk. Get to
understand You which is why they take the
time to listen instead speak. But us being
So large, so great in our own eyes,
We blow that person off.
We have no need for a new addition or so we
think. You see nowadays all we are focused on
Is where can I go, I meaning alone, I meaning
Not with you
Not with us
Me.
It's rare to find someone who thinks things like
How can I help You and how can We help
Them and how can They help Us help the
World get better. You see.
You see whatever happened to unity? What
happened to we're all in this TOGETHER?
What happened to All for One, One for All?
You see, we aren't looking at this right. So we
have access to the missing piece, which is
what? Unity. Abraham Lincoln once said "a
house divided amongst itself can not stand."
yet that has become our story. Not just Mine or

Yours it's OURS and we are indeed falling apart. Please don't leave people who care about you behind. Just because you move does not mean lose those you physically left. Whether we love or hate, we need to stay together because regardless of the situation love will take over. Now put that missing piece where it belongs...In our hearts.
Ask yourself, how can I change Me to We?

We must better ourselves in order to encourage others. The more we do that the more powerful the group becomes. Exchange the knife of hate and rejection for a fork of love and compassion so we can feed each other and be great.

Success

What is the meaning of success?
Is it money, cars, girls
Nothing more nothing less.
you don't have one of those
Your life's a mess
money is the only need to seem blessed
Clothes make up the best
What the heck
Is it all a test?
have we been shuffling the wrong deck?
Success...
Success...
Success?
Money, cars, girls
Nothing more nothing less
It's like life's success is based on bets
What if people focused on what's next
Never stopping on the most comfortable step
Money:first step
Cars:second step
Girls:third step
But does that have depth
Reaching for monetary gain
Is like the world's meth
But it doesn't matter as long as at least for a
second

We look the best.
It's one huge mess
Because the ladder of success
Is full at each and every step
Let me take this step
And state my meaning of success
Following your dreams,
that's success
Being yourself,
that's success
Being comfortable with you being you
That's success
Knowing life is more than what you have,
That's success
Growth through adversity
That's success
Feeling blessed even when life's a mess
That's success
Realizing that life isn't a one man thing and
reaching out to help others regardless the
situation
That's success
Moving on and going on and on and on after
failure
That's success
And finally learning to love others
That is true success
So ask yourself

What is the meaning of your success?

L.O.V.E

Learning
Of
Vulnerable
Engagement
Love
Wonderful gift from above
Fits us all like a magical glove
Except in times of trouble when we choose to
spill
Blood
Blood spilled over a tiny shove
Without knowing why it was done
Why not replace it with a hug
That rarely happens according to U.S gov
Where's the love?
What is love?
Love
It is
Recognizing the little things that make you
Beautiful
And valuing that they come from above
The many moments shared with others
To create a deeper bond
Is the best mode
Happiness and sacrifice
Like momma bear and her cub

So is love a dud?
Or is it more beautiful than a
Dove
What is love?
Learning
Of
Vulnerable
Engagement

Nature speaks

<u>Branchless tree</u>

Branchless tree
I guess that's me
Everyone tells me i'm free
But why does everything
seem out of
reach
At least I have feet
Too bad I can't move
What else did I lose
I guess i was always doomed
Because my branches never grew
What else is new
I always wished I was green
But i guess that will always remain a
dream
Life is as bad as can be
My brother grew one branch after
another
I could never blame my mother
It must be my roots down under
If only I push harder
Even if I become a martyr
I will have branches
Just a few more inches
I begin to hope
It becomes my only way to cope

I push and push
And all the sudden woosh
A branch has begun to form
I push and push
All the sudden woosh
Another branch as grown
Now i know I was never alone
Across the clearing I see my cousin
doing the same
Now i no longer feel like i was lame
I was just late entering the game
There's no one to blame
It was just my aim
Branchless tree
I guess that *was* me.

We may start off with no branches which
are goals we've reached, dreams
chased, or whatever you make them to
be. We have to know eventually we
have to rearrange our roots and dig
deeper within ourselves and believe
anything is possible then chase it. With
that branches will grow then leaves
thereafter.

<u>The thistle and thorn</u>

Thistles and thorns
They always warn
I can only look at them and scorn
It's just how they were born
It scares me to think
They could dwell on something
So beautiful, red and pink
Protection to the plant
Along withStyle
Distinction
Freedom
Strength
But
Disaster to the human
Along with
Useless
Unnecessary
Dangerous
Foolish
Who's right, the flower or the human?
Flowers are motionless and stuck in place.
The human is mobile and can move.
The flower has everything to lose
Human can keep their cool
Thistle and thorns that's just how
They were born.

Desert of Green

Desert of green
It's not what it seems
Abundance
is what it brings.
In its skies
Thousands of birds in the sky sing.
Growth is it's only gene
Power three times what anyone can believe.
Each plant plants its own seed
And it seems like the soil
Agrees.
Then comes the weed.
Hungry to satisfy its greedy
Needs
Desert of green
It's definitely not as it seems
It acts as if it breathes.
Tossing the leaves aside
To blow off steam.
The buzzing of bees
The sight of squirrels catching z's.
In minecraft they call the adventurer,
Steve.
Most people compare it to the sea.
Like waves it crashes the shore restlessly.

Who knows where it leads.
A land of new beasts?
A place where time flies at extraordinary
speed?
sigh
Desert of green
As endless as you may be
You flex wearing a completely
Different set of bling.

31

⊙Intermixed⊙

<u>Dreamer</u>

In the mind of dreamers
doubtless believers
Anything is possible
No matter how impossible,
Conceivable,
Attainable,
Explainable,
And
Valuable.
Nothing can stifle them
For their light is far from
Dim.
If society were a plant
They'd be the stem.
Who do you think learned how
To control the wind,
Make the chair you're
Sitting in.
What about this
Who made the
Phone,
Drone,
Even the clone.
Things you'd miss if they were
Gone.

How about who built your home
Learned how to mold stone.
Just look at how much the world has
Grown.
Yeah
They might have needed
A loan
But at least they know they earned
What they own,
The ones who stepped out the box
And said,
"It's time;
Time to wake up those creative thoughts."
Knock, knock.
The dreamer A.K.A the doubtless believer

River of dreams

They fill my mind everyday
In a time where it feels
All I can do is stay
Isolated in my minds cave
It's hard to feel brave
When no one else tries to do the same
Is everything I say game
Millions of these fill my mind with the question
Why was I made?
To get a good grade?
Be the king of spades?
It's hard enough being a different shade
My dreams became a debate
Laughter spread across every state
Isn't that great
Change
That's my dream and it won't let me escape
I cannot arrive late
Save my job for a different date
No thanks
Laugh now
because when I come up
it'll be too late
Just know I'm gonna be great
River of dreams fill my mind

Thrashing against the gates
Waiting to overflow and create
A beautiful place where a new being can stay
So who says I can't achieve my dreams
Don't hate
River of Dreams.

Silly Dream
It started off as a silly dream
I had no idea what this crazy thing would bring
Sometimes it feels like my head is full of
unnecessary steam
This dream had no industry
The sole purpose was to save you and me
At least that was my initial theme
At least?
Initial theme?
Yes, that's exactly what i mean
Because once i started chasing that dream
For whatever reason
Everyone thought it was best to laugh at me
My own parents looked disappointed to see
Their child beam
For accomplishing such a small step in
such a silly dream
My hope drained from me like water from
A dead sea
grass never looked less green
It was all over for what seemed
At least for me
A silly dream
Silly, silly dream
That word silly
Is a disgrace to me

Through chasing it I lost everything
What joy did it bring
Everyone doubted me
Except
Me

....

Except
Me

....

Hold up
How dare I let go of my dream
My silly, silly dream
How dare i let the people around me plant that
seed
That grew to make me do this crazy deed
Of killing my dream
To satisfy their need
To see me bleed
Oh please!
Silly dream?
Oh no
I'll show you the sheets
To prove to you that I, yeah I will
Succeed
Bound by you?
Oh no
I'm free.

And watch me turn this thing into a
masterpiece
Silly dream?
Oh yeah! That's all me!
Peace!

A Loner's Dream

A loner's dream is to be recognized
Be seen as something valuable in other's eyes
Hope the grass is greener on the other side
Well, lets just say to them that's a lie
Alone, they feel pushed aside
So from there they strive
For fame
To feel the same
Because people
once called them lame
What a shame
To quit the game for
monetary gain
Instead of change the game
For shame
A loner's dream is to be recognized
Well i wouldn't say all the time
Some decide to hide
While others wait for that moment to say "here
I rise"
Surprise
Forget all the lies
Because deep down inside
Resides
A light that once it shines…

Whoo whee
A loner's dream is to be recognized
Well that's a lie
A loner's true dream is to be free
That's what I decree
Be released
From doubt city
The depths of the self conscious sea
Anyone can agree
When you're set free
It's impossible not to believe
A loner's dream is not to be recognized
But for it to be realized
That from their "loneliness"
Happiness can arise.

Loners are never truly alone. They always
have a way of finding inspiration from the
things God puts into their hearts. Inspiration is
company and company is inspiration.

Colors

My skin is but a color
A color is not me
A tone shouldn't be so
Defining.
The only thing one can redeem
Is their place on the color
Scheme
Money can't buy what
People call the dream
Color
Black, white, yellow,red
Whatever it may be
Where does that definition lead
The sole determinant of
Many people's deeds
My skin is but a color
A color is not me
But every insult
Causes me to bleed
What does that
Mean
I don't always have the keys
As tragic as it seems
Not being a color
People try to bunch

me into their scheme
Kind,smart, well versed
Is just a theme in their eyes
I'm painted a different color
Entirely
Why does color have to be so defining?
My soul has many
But apparently no one cares to see
The beautiful mixtures within
Gleam
My skin is but a color
A color is not me.
Yes indeed.

Status

A king's crown represents his reign
If he walked in without it
Would his status be the same
with regular clothes
And a full grown mane
Would his subordinates know him by name?
Having lost his crown would another be made?
Throne never lost but
Distance the choice came
The people
Or throne
is it all a game
Something meant to stain
The image of he who reigns
A good king reigns
Feeding the poor with what he gains
Few are slain
For they all have a name
And provide important grain
One who treats them all the same
But if he came home would
Another crown be made?
Would he be forced to change
Because image is the name
of the game?

Would he become the person
Whom people pin the blame
When all happiness is drained?
Isn't that strange
To fill a position
One must mix in the range
Of happiness and gain
No need for a brain
No need to give a helping hand to the lame
Is that the throne a good king would
Want to gain?
If he were to return with
Regular clothes and
A mane
Would a new crown be made?
Would his status still
Be the same?

Internal bout

Sticks and stones
They,
They break my bones
At least until I realized
It was me all along
Being stuck all alone
In a place I can't call home
A broke off road
Now that's a load
Sticks and stones
They,
They break my bones
Realizing I'm all alone
Only recognized as someone else's
Clone
I'm forced to operate as a drone
That's why stones
Are the only clarity I've known
Simple
You pick it up and its thrown
Eventually enough hits will break bones
Like the happiness my anguish stole
Is there ever a goal
That doesn't have a pole
To interfere with the success of

He who is bold.
Sticks and stones
Yeah, they break my bones
Inside is where they've been for so long
On the outside you would never know
Sticks and stones rest inside tearing at my soul
What have I done so wrong
Is it my fault I'm alone
My oh my have I even grown
No positive ending to this
At least when *my* sticks and stones
Reside inside
To break my bones
Unlike those of those who build new homes.

<u>Idk</u>

We are but me and women
In a world of wonders and gems
But because our views are bent
What the world sees as gems
We see as cents
Cents=change
Change=difference
But In this case change is invaluable
Something meant to rest in a bottle
Until it has a whole dollars worth full
Beautiful wonders are seen as controllable
Where if we have no control it's destroyable
We do this to each other and it's horrible
How do we change destroyable to
understandable
How do we change controllable to joinable
And how do we change horrible to beautiful
It's not false news
It's not hatred
It's not continued false interpretation
It's not making one superior to the other
It's not killing to show dominance
It's not hating to endow fear
It's not destroying when things need to be built
It's not going back in time

These issues boil down to one simple solution
It requires L.O.V.E
I we loved what we have like a place to live
And people to share it with
If we loved where we could go
Then life wouldn't be such a tragedy show
If we learned to look at the gems we have
And the wonders down and back
We would realize
We are all but men and women in this world
and it's our job to help those things and each
other shine brighter.

All pieces were written and edited By
Emmanuel Wallace